Literary Neighborhoods of New York

Also in this series:

LITERARY
NEIGHBORHOODS
OF
NEW YORK

Marcia Leisner

STARRHILL PRESS
Washington & Philadelphia

Starrhill Press/publisher
P.O. Box 32342
Washington, DC 20007
(202) 686-6703

Illustrations by Jonel Sofian
Maps by Deb Norman

Library of Congress Cataloging in Publication Data

Leisner, Marcia
   Literary Neighborhoods of New York / Marcia Leisner. — 1st ed.
      p.   cm.
   Bibliography: p.
   Includes index.
   ISBN 0-913515-40-x : $7.95
   1. Literary landmarks—New York (N.Y.) 2. Authors, American—
Homes and haunts—New York (N.Y.) 3. American literature—
New York (N.Y.)—History and criticism. 4. New York (N.Y)—
Description—1981——Guide-books. 5. New York (N.Y.)—
Social life and customs. 6. New York (N.Y.)—Intellectual life.
I. Title.
PS144.N4L45   1989
917.47′1′04—dc19

88-34870
CIP

Printed in the United States of America
First edition
9 8 7 6 5 4 3 2 1

Contents

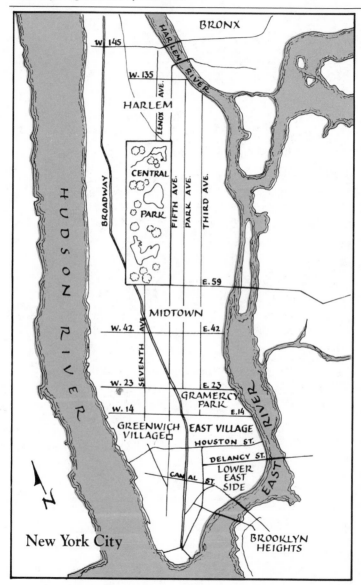

Introduction

"I love this dirty town!" cries Tony Curtis in *The Sweet Smell of Success*, one of the great movies about New York City. Clifford Odets, New York born and bred, wrote the line and he meant it. New York is dirty, crowded, noisy, tough, elegant, ugly and beautiful by turns and intensely romantic, a city of the imagination.

The writers who chose to live here, and most American writers, at least until recent years, have lived here at some period of their lives, did so because the city supplied what they needed. The publishers were here; intellectual life flourished; the arts were respected; the unconventional was accepted and the eccentric tolerated, even admired. Most of all there was the variety that only a great city can offer, and what city more than New York, the immigrants' town with its network of ethnic neighborhoods— Chinatown, Little Italy, Black Harlem, Spanish Harlem, the Jewish Lower East Side—each with its own character, its customs, its restaurants, its celebrations? O. Henry, William Dean Howells, Stephen Crane, Henry James were all walkers in the city, poking into new neighborhoods in search of the writer's specialty: the complexities of human existence.

Old neighborhoods are changing, swept away by housing projects, ethnic migrations, and the high cost of living in Manhattan. Aspiring newcomers are outpriced. Future Edna Millays look elsewhere for a place to live.

This book is designed to fit into your pocket or pocketbook. It covers seven New York neighborhoods, each with a particularly rich literary heritage. Subway transportation information appears at the beginning of each chapter. Walking times will vary according to your pace and your interest in the neighborhood but need never exceed two hours. Occasionally, I have mentioned eating places along the way, but only when the atmosphere and the cuisine express the spirit of their highly individualized surroundings. I hope you will enjoy exploring these neighborhoods while they are still yours to explore.

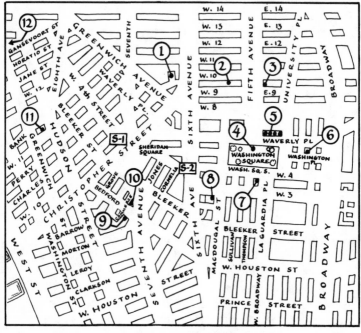

Greenwich Village

1. 4 Patchin Place (E. E. Cummings)
2. 14 W. 10th Street (Mark Twain)
3. 21 Fifth Avenue (Mark Twain, later)
4. Arch at Washington Square
5. Setting for Henry James's *Washington Square*
6. Site of Henry James's birthplace, 21 Washington Place
7. Site of the "genius houses"
8. Minetta Tavern
9. 75 Bedford Street (Edna St. Vincent Millay)
10. Chumley's Bar, 86 Bedford Street
    (no sign, just a huge oak door)
11. White Horse Tavern
12. Gansevoort Street Pier

Greenwich Village

"PLEASE, WHERE can I find the wild bohemians?" an innocent visitor will occasionally still ask on a Village street. Where, indeed? Gone with the snows of yesteryear.

Greenwich Village—*The* Village—is now inhabited by doctors, lawyers and other people who can pay the high rents. Unknown artists and assorted free spirits would like to live in this delightful, convenient neighborhood, but unless they have an independent income or have latched on to that increasingly rare phenomenon, a rent-controlled apartment, they must go elsewhere. The hip-looking young people you see on the streets are often tourists.

The bohemian society of the 1920s and 1930s is only one chapter in the history of the Village. The neighborhood is, and always has been, a cross-section of New York. The Dutch drove out the Indians. Rich merchants moved in. Italian immigrants took over the streets south of Washington Square, where their descendants still live. Tom Paine spent his last years here; Edgar Allen Poe helped run a rooming house at 113½ Carmine Street; Henry James was born near Washington Square. Before World War I, the people soon to be lumped together as "bohemians" flocked in because rents were cheap.

This is perhaps New York's most charming neighborhood to wander in. Skip 8th Street, the main drag, unless you are looking for shoes, junk food or crowds. The streets west of Sheridan Square are more interesting, lined with fine and not so fine old houses, boutiques, restaurants, coffee shops and antique shops. On week-ends, Washington Square Park is bedlam: guitar players around the fountain, mothers with baby carriages on benches, and, until recently, an army of crack dealers to greet you as you passed under the mighty arch.

There is still plenty to see and enjoy. What has gone is the vital presence of the poets and painters who created the city's one central art quarter.

HENRY JAMES (1843–1916) was a Greenwich Village boy, born at 21 Washington Place just east of Washington Square, which furnishes the title and the setting for one of his best-known novels. Catherine Sloper, the unfortunate heroine, lived in one of the splendid town houses that line the north side and was courted by her faithless lover on a bench in the square. You may remember Olivia De Havilland as Catherine in the movie, *The Heiress*, made from the novel. Most of the Washington Square North houses now belong to New York University, a major property holder in the Village and loved about as much as major property holders usually are.

James belonged to a family which is to American letters what the Adams family is to American politics. His father, Henry Sr., was a philosopher, lecturer and essayist; his brother William a philosopher, author of *Varieties of Religious Experience*. The children were privately educated, brought up to be independent thinkers, cosmopolitan in outlook. The family traveled extensively in the leisurely way of well-off nineteenth-century families. Henry (Henry James, Jr., as he was known in early life) put in some time at Harvard Law School and began to contribute to American journals. He made Cambridge, Massachusetts, his headquarters, but Europe drew him. In 1875, he moved to Paris and the next year to London, which became his permanent home. It was a good observation post for what was to become his major subject: Americans abroad, caught in the clash between old and new civilizations. He, himself, fitted in. During one London season he accepted 107 invitations (how many did he turn down?). In spite of his full social life, he could be lonely. One winter evening, so he told a friend, he stood outside a house looking up at the friendly lighted windows and wept. He never married, apparently never had love affairs with women. Choice? Homosexuality? A mysterious carriage accident which rendered him impotent? Nobody knows.

Shortly before he died, and in an excess of World War I sympathy for England, James became a British citizen. He left behind a tremendous body of work. His reputation for being hard to read is, like the rumors of Mark Twain's death, exaggerated. True, the paragraph-long sentences in some of his later novels— *The Golden Bowl* in particular—require concentration. Otherwise, he is most approachable: quite gothic and scary when he wants to be, moving, always acute, and entertaining. He is one of the last masters of the classic novel form.

WILLA CATHER (1873–1947) came to New York via rural Virginia, small-town Nebraska, and Pittsburgh. She was thirty-one years old with a career as teacher and journalist and a book of poems, *April Twilights*, to her credit when S. S. McClure hired her as an editor for his prestigious *McClure's* magazine.

She took a place at 60 Washington Square South, one of the so-called "genius houses." These were seedy but atmospheric studios inhabited at various times by other writers—Theodore Dreiser, O. Henry, Stephen Crane—now replaced by the pseudo-Colonial buildings of The New York University Law School. Years later she set a bittersweet love story, "Coming, Aphrodite!" (in her short story collection, *Youth and the Bright Medusa*) in these bohemian surroundings.

Cather soon moved to a more comfortable apartment in a brownstone at 5 Bank Street (also demolished), where she lived for years with her companion and chronicler, Edith Lewis. She rose to the position of managing editor of *McClure's*, then resigned to write full time.

Much of Willa Cather's life is in her books. She became a great literary light but never an international celebrity like Mark Twain nor a symbol for her generation like Edna Millay. She had no interest in the social ferment of her times. A young friend, a settlement house worker, tried to interest her in the problems of the Italian immigrants who crowded the narrow streets—MacDougal, Thompson, Sullivan—behind Washington Square South but was met with polite indifference. The Sacco-Vanzetti case, which rocked literary New York in the 1920s, drew no reaction from her. She never quite comprehended social activism or the need for organized protest. For her, the solution lay in self-help, the sturdy independence of the Western pioneers she had known in her youth. These were the people she understood and wrote about in *My Ántonia, O Pioneers!, Death Comes for the Archbishop, The Song of the Lark.*

One thing that *did* move her was music. She started out as a passionate Wagnerian. Her friendship with the American Wagnerian soprano, Olive Fremstad, who like the people Cather most admired was a small-town Westerner as well as a great artist, inspired *The Song of the Lark,*—"the most convincing story of artist life written by an American," says literary historian Vernon Parrington. When she met the Menuhins, violin prodigy Yehudi and his two talented, intellectual little sisters, it was instant friendship. She became "Aunt Willa." Together they formed a Shakespeare club, and her musical taste ripened to include Schubert lieder and the great works of Beethoven.

Heroic and independent, like one of her own heroines, Cather never stopped writing. Her publisher, Alfred Knopf, once compared her to certain younger writers who had to be curried and combed and brought to the starting line by their editors: "With Willa it was different. She would write me that she had a new book. The manuscript would arrive, and that was it." She was planning another novel and another Western trip when she died.

HERMAN MELVILLE (1819–1891) has left his imprint all over lower Manhattan, but the best place to recall the tragedy of the author of *Moby-Dick* is at the Gansevoort Street pier on the western outskirts of the Village, opposite the wholesale meat market.

It's a sad, autumnal scene: the empty harbor, the decaying pier with its collapsed shed and junked cars, the grim pile of the City Department of Sanitation with its crematorium chimney next door. Here, Melville spent nineteen years as an outdoor customs inspector—"a most inglorious vocation," he called his job.

Melville was not the transplanted New Englander one might think from reading *Moby-Dick* but a native New Yorker born at 6 Pearl Street in lower Manhattan. His mother was a member of an old Dutch family (ironically, the Gansevoorts) married to a member of an old New England family. Allan Melville died early, leaving his family penniless. Maria Gansevoort Melville, a cold, proud woman, very much caught up in her distinguished ancestry, suffered her new poverty intensely. She took no pleasure in her passionate, romantic son. It was a deeply scarring relationship. Herman went off to sea when he was eighteen, and ended it. "Call me Ishmael," *Moby-Dick* begins. Call me outcast.

Out of Melville's sea experience came two highly successful novels, *Typee* and *Omoo*. He married, fathered a family, bought a farm in the Berkshires. Then came *Moby-Dick*, the book that ruined him financially and emotionally. The critics excoriated it; the public ignored it. It was his nemesis, just as the White Whale was Captain Ahab's. Only during the 1920s was it rediscovered and elevated to its rightful stature.

Melville's later books failed to please anyone. *Pierre*, a wild, fierce novel incorporating murder, incest and suicide, shocked the few who read it. *The Confidence Man*, a savage attack on commercial society, made little impression on the public. After this book, Melville withdrew into silence. "He informed me that he had pretty much made up his mind to be annihilated," writes Nathaniel Hawthorne's son, Julian. "Herman has taken to writing poetry," his wife wrote her mother in 1859. "Don't tell anyone, you know how things get around."

And so Herman Melville went down to oblivion, plodding through his days at the customs shed until his wife inherited some money and he was able to retire. *Billy Budd,* so admired by modern readers, was found among his papers after he died.

The family buried him in a modest grave in Woodlawn Cemetery in the Bronx with a blank scroll for a monument. The *New York Times* obituary remarked that he had won considerable fame by the publication in 1847 of a book entitled *Typee.*

MARK TWAIN (1835–1910), born Samuel Langhorne Clemens, was an immensely peripatetic man. The Clemens family went everywhere, lived in a variety of American and European cities. In 1900 he took a year's lease on a spacious brownstone at 14 West 10th Street, just west of Fifth Avenue. A second, and terrible, fame descended on the building in 1987 when six-year-old Lisa Steinberg was beaten to death in her adoptive parents' third floor apartment.

In 1900, Mark Twain was at the pinnacle of his success, one of the most famous, most quoted, most courted persons in the world. At sixty-five he was as vital and gregarious as ever. He was rich and lived in baronial style, entertaining lavishly, playing billiards with all comers, still "the belle of New York", as he had once described himself to his wife.

She was Olivia Langdon—"Livy"—a genteel lady from Elmira, New York. Over the years she had tamed the former printer's apprentice, riverboat pilot, miner and itinerant journalist and had transformed him into devoted husband and paterfamilias, full-time celebrity and part-time writer. He adored her in the 19th-century manner, as a superior being—so pale, delicate and suffering. She adored him back and undertook his re-education, upgrading him to her standards by censoring his neckties (he had always worn a Western string tie; she got him into cravats), his strong language and his prose. *Huckleberry Finn,* his masterwork, rather embarrassed her. She and the girls preferred *The Prince and the Pauper.*

In 1904, after more wandering, he came back to New York, renting a showplace at 21 Fifth Avenue, corner of 9th Street. This majestic brownstone, designed in neo-Gothic style by James

Renwick, the architect who had done Grace Church (Broadway at 10th Street), was demolished in the philistine 1950s, despite protests, to make way for an undistinguished apartment house.

The Clemens family had been sadly reduced by Livy's death. The bright beloved youngest daughter Susy had died in 1896. Clara was ill. Only Jean remained at home with "Papa." He didn't go out much any more but stayed at home to write intermittently.

Just as he bore the dual name of Clemens-Twain, he carried inside himself a dual nature. He was never able to reconcile the two. One side dominated in the golden happiness of Part I of *Life on the Mississippi*, the other in the savage despair of his late novel, *The Mysterious Stranger*. Aided and abetted by Livy, hungry for fame and money, Mark Twain squandered his incomparable gifts. Livy's pet name for him was "Youth." "What a child he was—to the end!" writes his biographer, Albert Bigelow Paine. How he loved the limelight, dressing up, living it up! And what a toll that took on his writing. The old frontiersman got lost along the way.

Mark Twain was a casualty of his age—the Gilded Age—that era of industrial robber barons, overdecorated houses, overdressed women and general crassness. From a teeming imagination he has left four masterpieces: *Huckleberry Finn*, *Tom Sawyer*, the first part of *Life on the Mississippi* and *The Mysterious Stranger;* no American writer has surpassed him when he was at his best.

No. 75 Bedford Street, a three-story dollhouse only 9½ feet wide, is known as the Millay House. And, indeed, **EDNA ST. VINCENT MILLAY** (1892–1950) did live here for a short time but only at the end of her meteoric Village career.

If any one person symbolizes bohemian Greenwich Village, it is Millay. Her poems spoke for the "new woman" who emerged after World War I, freed from corsets, long skirts and long hair, independent as a young man, challenging conventions and greedy for life.

Millay was a Maine girl, the eldest of three sisters, and a Vassar graduate, class of 1917. Fame came early with her long poem,

"Renascence," which did *not* win the $500 prize offered in 1912 by the anthology, *The Lyric Year.* Her failure was something of a cause célèbre—even the winner felt the prize was rightfully hers. She came to the Village after graduation, a minor celebrity hoping for a stage career. A small part in a Theatre Guild production came her way; then nothing. After a cold and hungry winter in a furnished room at 138 Waverly Place, she was joined by her sisters. They took an apartment at 25 Charlton Street, and life really began.

The Millay girls caused a sensation in the Village. Everybody was in love with at least one of them, and especially with Edna. She was fascinating, no doubt about that. Red-gold hair, green eyes, a flair for clothes—but not a certified beauty. She could be quite plain at times—a mouse in a corner—until the mood overtook her and she spoke out in that rich, vibrant voice, so amazing issuing from such a small body.

For several years and with half a dozen suitors, Millay hesitated on the brink of matrimony, always drawing back at the last moment because she felt domesticity wouldn't work for her. She was a sort of American Sappho, writing passionately and frankly about love: the many lips she had kissed, the arms that had lain under her head till morning. What she didn't mention was that in those mornings, she inevitably retreated into her work. That came first. For all their gaiety and unconventionality, Millay and her Village writer friends were a serious, hard-working lot, rumors of orgies to the contrary.

Then, when she was thirty-one, she found a man with whom marriage would work. Eugen Boissevain, a Dutch coffee merchant and the widower of a well-known feminist, Iris Mulholland, understood perfectly that Millay's job was to write, his to run the house and protect her from an increasingly invasive world. Few women have had such luck or such pampering.

They lived in the little Bedford Street house for a year before buying Steepletop, a 700-acre farm in upstate New York. Millay had become the best-known, most-quoted poet in the country. With book royalties and poetry-reading tours she was making money, but New York with its crowds and noise oppressed her. She was thirty-three when she pulled up stakes. The rest of her life was divided between Steepletop and an island off the coast of Maine that she and Boissevain bought. This most Villagey of poets spent only eight years in the neighborhood.

A poignant little postscript, added by an old friend, describes a Millay visit to her old haunts. She is seated alone in the back of an open touring car, with Boissevain at the wheel. Slowly they drive through the familiar Village streets, Millay devouring everything with her eyes. The queen returning to the kingdom she had abdicated.

E. E. CUMMINGS (1894–1962) lived at 4 Patchin Place from 1924 to the end of his life. There's something so charming about coming upon this little mews with its iron gates and its ailanthuses—city weed trees—just a few steps down Tenth Street west of noisy Sixth Avenue. The gates aren't locked; you can walk in and look around. Nothing pretentious about the place—the houses are small and undistinguished—but it's so quiet here. A nice place for a poet who always loved nature.

Edward Estlin Cummings, called "Estlin" (his father was the Edward of the family), was born in Cambridge, Massachusetts, son of a Harvard professor and Unitarian minister. He graduated from Harvard, where he majored in the classics, made many literary-minded friends who remained his friends, and began to make a reputation as a poet.

His individual style—all those lowercase letters that have led people to write about "e. e. cummings," the irregularly spaced lines, the seemingly arbitrary capitalization of words—began to emerge after much experimenting with the family typewriter. Such departures from accepted form could, he began to realize, indicate or heighten meaning and emotion. That he was also a painter is important. The placement of the printed word on the page had special meaning for him. He *saw* the words as he wrote them. Absence of punctuation could create interesting ambiguities. He would free himself from poetry's formal bonds and avoid what he called the "hot house" language too many poets found suitable for "elevated" thoughts.

In 1917, after Harvard, young Cummings, who was a pacifist, joined the ambulance service and went to France. There he shortly got into bad trouble. Indiscreet though harmless letters written by him and a friend and associate, resulted in his being accused by the French government of spying for the Germans. He was interned for months in a government camp for deserters. This was a big adventure for a boy who had always lived the quiet and privileged life of a middle-class American student. He wrote his distracted parents that he was having the time of his life. He changed his mind about that when he got scurvy. His parents got him released, somewhat the worse for the experience. Out of this time, however, came his book, *The Enormous Room*, a landmark World War I novel.

Ironically, Cummings was drafted shortly after his return from France. He spent a boring and irksome year in the army before being discharged, still, and to his great satisfaction, plain Private Cummings.

He was an attractive man, blond but with Tartar cheekbones and slanting eyes, a big talker and an entertaining one, playing with words as he did in his poems. Women liked him. He married three times, always beauties.

It's not pleasant to think of him as he grew older. First his health began to fail, then his temper. The lively, social man became reclusive and difficult—a "curmudgeon," one of his friends remembers him in those years. Politically he moved to the far right, first as a hater of "that man in the White House" (Roosevelt), eventually as a supporter of Joseph McCarthy, gleefully agreeing with the senator's attacks on Harvard. One of his later poems could easily be interpreted as an anti-Semitic diatribe, although he vigorously denied any such intention.

DYLAN THOMAS (1914–1953) made four reading tours in the United States. They resembled rock star tours—no dope, but floods of booze, groupies, fans and afterwards, the legend.

By the time he arrived in New York, the Welsh poet was no longer the curly-headed angel of his youth but a paunchy, popeyed man, much the worse for drink but with his creative power still in full force.

In Thomas the famous Celtic temperament—lyrical, passionate and romantic—was in full bloom. He was a tremendous talker and raconteur, always the center of attention in the pubs and bars where he spent half his life "singing for his supper," his wife, the beautiful, tempestuous, long-suffering Caitlin writes. In New York he felt at home in the midtown Irish bars, but above all he preferred the Village bars: the San Remo on MacDougal Street, last outpost of a disappearing bohemia, and the White Horse on Hudson Street, where they still point out his regular table.

He was a tiny creature, only about 5 feet, 2 inches tall, but with a great voice that came booming out of nowhere and a dramatic talent big enough to have served a stage actor. It is easy to understand why his readings drew such crowds. Recordings will give you an idea of the spell he cast.

To judge Dylan Thomas as a professional bad boy, a lecher with a habit of propositioning women in four-letter words, a house guest who stole his host's shirts, is to ignore the sober, serious poet whose true involvement was with his muse. "He had a romantic view of the poet as rebel," Caitlin writes, "A very conventional perception and an old-fashioned one." America may have turned his head with its adulation, but it did not corrupt his verse.

He died of the drink in St. Vincent's Hospital in the Village. Crowds gathered outside; fans held candlelight vigils. Inside, Caitlin, who had been summoned from England, broke down and had to be temporarily committed to Bellevue. Thomas was thirty-nine—the same age as Byron. A romantic to the end, he believed that good poets die young, and he did.

GREENWICH VILLAGE BARS & CHARACTERS. When Greenwich Village became notorious as the Latin Quarter of the New World, the double-decker Fifth Avenue buses began to bring downtown hordes of sightseers eager to observe the bohemians in their natural habitats. This was easy enough because the long-haired men and short-haired women loved to congregate and talk—first in such tearooms(!) as Polly's on MacDougal Street, Romany Marie's on Washington Square South (run for years by a self-styled gypsy), or the Jumble Shop on 8th Street, which lingered on until the 1970s as a staid restaurant. During Prohibition, speakeasies proliferated. Repeal saw the rise of such bars as the San Remo and the Minetta Tavern on MacDougal Street, Chumley's (a former discreet speak) on Bedford Street, the White Horse on Hudson. These, with the exception of the Remo, are still in place. Their clientele is now college students, suburbanites, a few neighborhood people, and occasional aging survivors from the wreckage of bohemia.

JOE GOULD—Joseph Ferdinand Gould, Harvard 1911—was a fixture in Village bars and cafeterias during the 1940s and 1950s. "The last of the bohemians," as he called himself, was a scrawny little man with a beard and no fixed address. He slept in Bowery flophouses, on park benches, on a friend's floor. Bartenders called him "Professor." For a drink, he would flap his arms and imitate the caw of a gull, which earned him the second name of "Professor Seagull." Under his arm he always carried a portfolio containing his life's work, *An Oral History of Our Time.* The manuscript, written in longhand in copybooks, ran to millions of words. Joe Gould took notes on everything—overheard conversations, Village parties, strange things seen on nightlong walks through the city; there were essays on his various interests and obsessions: the zipper as a sign of decadence, fleas, cafeteria cooking. "I have fully cover-ed the intellectual underworld of my time," Gould said. Whether he was a sort of Samuel Pepys of the Bowery, as his friend, poet Horace Gregory, believed, or whether *Oral History* was merely a massive confusion of words, no one knows. The notebooks disappeared with Gould's death in 1954 and have never been found. *An Oral History of Our Time* remains a literary mystery.

MAXWELL BODENHEIM'S life is a bohemian cautionary tale—wine, women and poetry, with all the dire results usually prophesied. In between the sorry beginning and the sorry end, he may have had a good time.

Born poor in Mississippi and badly educated, he made his way to Chicago to be a poet. After conquering bohemian Chicago, he moved in the 1920s to Greenwich Village: a golden-haired, "Christlike" figure with plenty of sex appeal, especially for the thrill-seeking girls who populated the fringes of literary life. His poetry was good enough to be published in magazines and anthologies; he wrote a sexy, best-selling novel, *Replenishing Jessica.* Unlike his contemporary, Joe Gould, he ventured into the big world and made it.

His decline was rapid and fearful. From poet and homme fatal, for whom girls attempted, and in one case succeeded in committing suicide, he sank to drink-cadger in Village bars. He was murdered one night in 1954 in a room off the Bowery, together with his current lover, but no friend came forward to testify against the murderer at his trial. Max had died long before.

Washington Square Arch

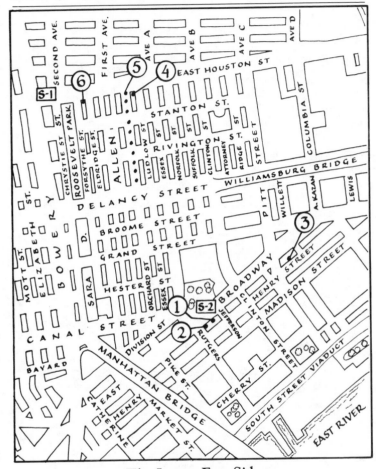

The Lower East Side

1. Former home of the *Jewish Daily Forward*
2. Site of the Garden Cafeteria
3. 265 Henry Street, Henry Street Settlement House
4. Katz's Delicatessen
5. Orchard Street shopping area
6. Yonah Schimmel Knish Bakery

The Jewish Lower East Side

Subway Stops: S-1. Second Avenue (IND F train)
S-2. East Broadway (IND F train)

THE OLD Lower East Side with its narrow, tenement-lined streets was the first New York home for generations of Jewish immigrants from Eastern Europe.

Life in the ghetto was hard for the newcomers: terrible poverty, sweatshop labor, "cold water" (heatless) flats, rampant TB, crime. Only the strongest survived. How many died or returned, beaten and disillusioned with the "Golden Land," no one knows. Their stories are lost, stifled by familiar success stories: Eddie Cantor, George Burns, Al Jolson, Sid Caesar, George Gershwin.

This great human drama provided a natural laboratory for writers. Journalists, novelists and poets recorded the life around them in all its aspects. Outsiders came to observe the phenomenon. Henry James was alarmed by the crude vitality of what he called "The Yiddish World," so different from and so threatening to his genteel New York. Henry Adams was moved to outright anti-Semitism. Jacob Riis photographed and wrote an accurate, if carefully distanced, study of the community, *How the Other Half Lives*. Lillian Wald, a well-bred young woman from Rochester, came to stay, first as a visiting nurse, then as founder and head resident of the Henry Street Settlement, still at 265 Henry Street.

As the old Lower East Side recedes into the past, its legend grows. Sentimental memory, suffering from *Fiddler on the Roof* disease, pictures it as a quaint folk community. Quaint it was not; interesting, fascinating—yes, but more interesting, more fascinating to those who did not have to live in the tenements. The ones who did wanted out. One must add, however, that former residents are never able to forget the old neighborhood. They love it and hate it. Such is the power of this extraordinary place.

Today's Lower East Side still qualifies as a slum, although entire blocks of tenements have been demolished for housing projects (the latest in slums). The Jews have largely gone. In their place are newer immigrants, most of them Hispanic. A few streets have retained their lively grand bazaar quality. Orchard Street is still a famous shopping street, but now it sells discount designer fashions, jeans and running shoes instead of pickles and "half a quarter" of butter.

The Orchard Street neighborhood (IND F train, Second Avenue stop) has two typical places to eat. At Katz's Delicatessen, East Houston Street, corner of Ludlow, take a ticket and proceed to the cafeteria counter. Corned beef and pastrami are the specialties. Also such local beverages as Dr. Brown's Cel-Ray (celery flavor) tonic. No coffee! Order tea with lemon in a glass.

At Yonah Schimmel Knish Bakery, 137 East Houston Street, between Forsyth and Eldrich Streets, customers have been coming in since 1910 for potato or kasha knishes, homemade yogurt and other vegetarian delicacies produced by this unassuming but most revered of bakeries. Don't be turned off by the humble interior. And don't forget to look for the faded photograph of the original Mr. Schimmel in the window: a bit of old Lower East Sideiana preserved.

THE JEWISH DAILY FORWARD (IND F train, East Broadway stop). The tall building at 175 East Broadway, the Park Avenue of the old ghetto and still a handsome street, was until recently the headquarters of the *Jewish Daily Forward*, once the largest Yiddish-language daily newspaper in the world. It still exists, under sadly reduced circumstances, at 45 East 33rd Street.

Its long-time editor, **ABRAHAM CAHAN** (1860–1951), was a brilliant journalist and, like his readers, an immigrant who had been through the painful Americanization process. Under his dictatorship, which lasted from 1902 until his death, the *Forward* evolved from a low-circulation Socialist paper into a neighborhood institution. From his pulpit on the editorial page, Cahan regularly sermonized his readers: "Educate the Children!", "Learn English!", "Organize a Union!" In brief: pull yourself up by your bootstraps and make it in the New Land.

Left-wingers detested Cahan for his moderate, conciliatory Socialism, and undoubtedly many of his staff members disliked him, for he was a cranky, opinionated man, very difficult to work for. Whatever his limitations, he knew his readers and cared about them. Nowhere is this more apparent than in "A Bintel Brief" ("Bundle of Letters"), the paper's "Dear Abbie" column. This feature was Cahan's brainchild, and at first he wrote all the pithy, commonsensical and stern answers—and sometimes the letters as well. "Honored Editor," they inevitably begin, and then the problem: a deserted wife, an unruly daughter, a fiancée with dimples (bad luck in the old country). What a picture these letters give of immigrant life! How fortunate that a collection in translation (compiled by Isaac Metzker; Garden City, 1971) has been published.

Like many another journalist, Cahan had novelistic yearnings. He did manage one successful novel. In 1917, *The Rise of David Levinsky* was published to both critical and financial success. He wrote the book in English, and it is to this day one of the most complete and accurate, though somewhat plodding, studies of the immigrant saga to be found.

The *Forward* followed the old world newspaper custom of printing short stories and serializing novels. Long before he was published in English, let alone considered for the Nobel Prize, ISAAC BASHEVIS SINGER (1904–   ) was well known to *Forward* readers.

His is an interesting story. Born in Galicia, the heartland of Polish-Russian Jewry, he was taken to Warsaw as a small child, hence his *Forward* pen name, Isaac Warshawsky. Son of a rabbi and descended on both sides from rabbis, he grew up in the heart of

Warsaw's Jewish quarter, steeped in Jewish lore and tradition. *In My Father's Court* recaptures the atmosphere. Eavesdropping from a corner of his father's study, he overheard many curious stories which he later used in his fiction. His intelligence destined him for the rabbinical life, but his interests were decidedly secular. He followed his brother Israel, already a writer, into the bohemian life of Warsaw. Then with the advent of Nazism, he followed his brother to America. Israel Joshua Singer died too soon, leaving two splendid novels, *The Brothers Ashkenazi* and *Yoshe Kalb.* What would have happened if he had been able to continue writing?

Isaac Bashevis eventually went to work for the *Forward* but lived in Brooklyn, not the Lower East Side. Today, he lives on West 86th Street, and until a few years ago could be found in the Manhattan phone book and telephoned by anybody. What might be out of the question for a rock star worked for a writer: calls he received from strangers led to adventures, many of which he translated into fiction.

Singer, the man and the writer, is a magician, an enchanter. Witty and profound, he first enthralled a non-Yiddish-speaking audience with his Nobel Prize acceptance speech, and later, mass audiences when Dick Cavett interviewed him on TV. He still lectures occasionally at the 92nd Street YMHA (92nd Street and Lexington Avenue, a great New York cultural spa). He writes about demons (with his bald head, pointed, projecting ears, and lively eyes, he resembles one of his creations), small town and big city types, con men and rabbis, summoning up a world destroyed by the Holocaust in a heady blend of realism, fantasy, folklore and Freud. When he changes his scene to New York (or to Miami or South America, as he does now that he lectures in many cities where Jews abound), he puts the same ingredients into fictional play. The *New Yorker* publishes many of his short stories, which says a good deal about his wide appeal.

As you turn back from the *Forward* building to Rutgers Street, note the Chinese Restaurant at the corner. For years, this was the

Garden Cafeteria, meeting place for writers. Those plate glass windows made good observation posts. Singer himself might have come upon an idea or two gazing out over the steam rising from his glass of tea.

By the 1920s the younger generation—the second generation—born in America or brought here young, had begun to write about their experience. Life for them was a struggle as hard as their parents', but in a different way.

ANZIA YEZIERSKA (born in Poland in the 1880s, died 1970) has been resurrected by the new interest in forgotten women writers. All seven of her books (*Bread Givers, Hungry Hearts* and *The Open Cage* are back in print) deal with the conflict between the generations from a woman's point of view. The young struggle with old-world, religious parents; the old, with Americanized children who have discarded the past. Economics plays a major role for both generations: the young are sweatshop-bound every bit as much as their parents, but their ambitions are American. They want and they fight for everything the New Country has to offer. A painful assimilation.

SAMUEL ORNITZ (1891–1957) got himself a best seller in *Haunch, Paunch and Jowl.* Published in 1923 as an "anonymous autobiography," it went into twelve printings. Crudely written but compelling, it is the familiar story of the rise of an East Side boy from the tenements to "All Rightniks Row," Riverside Drive, the promised land of aspiring Jews. Why "anonymous"? Perhaps because it describes the criminal underworld of the ghetto and the corruption of Tammany Hall. Perhaps it was too frank (for those times) about the life inside the cold flats. More likely because "anonymous" spelled "spicy" to readers and to the slummers who invaded poor neighborhoods en masse. The ignoble entertainment of slumming flourished during the 1920s and was by no means peculiar to the Lower East Side. Harlem suffered even more from incursions of sightseers eager to find out how the other half lived. In downtown Manhattan, pedestrians still thumb their noses at sight-seeing busses.

The "proletarian novel," a term popularized by Marxist critics to describe fiction carrying the message of class-conscious socialism, emerged full-force during the Depression years of the 1930s when so many intellectuals joined or sympathized with the Communist Party and expected the Revolution momentarily.

MICHAEL GOLD'S *Jews Without Money,* an autobiographical account of growing up in the tenements, was a "proletarian" best seller in 1930, the year of the great debacle. It ends with a paean for the coming Revolution, which was to have turned the East Side into a garden, thus establishing its right to the genre. Sentimental it may be, but it is still a tremendously powerful evocation of the old neighborhood: "Always those faces at the tenement windows. The street never failed them. It was an immense excitement. It never slept. It roared like the sea. It exploded like fireworks."

About Mike Gold (1893–1967): he was born Ytsaach Granich, but changed his name to Michael Gold—such a romantic, working-class sort of name—to evade the Palmer Raids, anti-radical sweeps of the 1920s. He was no painfully self-educated man but a smart kid who went to Harvard for a year and dropped out for lack of funds. Back in New York he became a member of the left wing intelligentsia, an editor of the very influential Communist weekly, *The New Masses,* and for years a columnist on *The Daily Worker. The Hollow Men,* a collection of his criticism, most of it reprinted from the *Worker,* shows him at his most doctrinaire, giving hell to T. S. Eliot, Joyce, O'Neill and "bourgeois" writers in general.

HENRY ROTH (1906–   ), unlike the other East Side writers, is a stylist. His sole novel, *Call It Sleep,* (1934), was admired by all except the Communist critics. "Too introspective. . . . Young writers have better things to do with working class experience."

Roth, who was himself a Communist, withdrew to a farm in Maine and literary silence. In 1964, *Call It Sleep* was reissued to immediate acclaim.

The book is a picture of the Lower East Side seen through a child's eyes. Savage, mysterious, dangerous; a neighborhood populated by the uprooted and the lost—no kindly folk characters here. In the streets, communication is through a hideous, deformed English—"caveman talk," a recent critic has called it. At home, civilization reinstates itself in the elegant, flowing mother tongue of Yiddish. A stunning literary performance, the high point of East Side writing.

Orchard Street

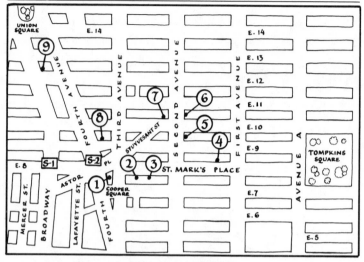

The East Village

1. Great Hall of Cooper Union
2. Site of James Fenimore Cooper's house at No. 6
3. St. Mark's Bookshop
4. 77 St. Mark's Place (W. H. Auden)
5. Second Avenue Delicatassen
6. Site of the Café Royal
7. St. Mark's Church-in-the-Bowery (Poetry Project)
8. Pageant Book & Print Co.
9. Strand Book Store

The East Village

Subway Stops: How to get there: BMT local (RR) to 8th Street, or Lexington Avenue IRT No.6 train to Astor Place.

UNTIL THE 1960s, the East Village was simply one of the many neighborhoods that made up the Lower East Side, a Polish and Ukrainian enclave in the Jewish district. When Greenwich Village rents began to soar, real estate agents looked eastward and discovered new possibilities in the streets beyond Astor Place. A new name, one that would effectively dissociate the neighborhood from the Lower East Side (slumland), was necessary. Hence, East Village. Respectable but—that new adjective which was replacing "bohemian"—hip.

New York's first big disco, the Electric Circus, opened in a cavernous electric-blue building, formerly the Polish National Home, on St. Mark's Place. The Beautiful People, who had been invented at the same time as the East Village, flocked in. *Vogue* covered the fashions and the goings-on. The Fillmore East on Second Avenue at 6th Street began its career as a Rock Palace. Hordes of hippies ("hipsters" they were called at the time) and druggies converged on the scene. Old-timers were dismayed. Many fled, many were pushed out. The transformation took root.

The East Village today is a neighborhood of violent contrasts and strong opinions: homeless men and women sleeping in doorways and living in Tompkins Square Park, the scene of a bloody battle with the police during the summer of '88; the serene old New York atmosphere of Stuyvesant Street with its landmark houses; crowds of tourists gawking at fantastically-dressed street people; peddlers clogging the sidewalks with their dilapidated wares; well-tailored briefcase carriers hurrying to work; petition gatherers for every imaginable cause on the corner of Second Avenue and St. Mark's Place.

COOPER UNION. Standing on the island of Cooper Square at the gates of the newly christened East Village is the huge brownstone bulk of the Great Hall of Cooper Union.

Founded in 1859 by **PETER COOPER**, reformer, philanthropist, benevolent (as opposed to robber baron) capitalist, to help the working man educate himself, Cooper Union's free lectures have for more than a century provided a forum for free speech and social reform. Abraham Lincoln lectured here. "Louder, louder!" the audience yelled. Lincoln turned up the volume and won himself a presidential nomination. Mark Twain, Harriet Beecher Stowe and many other Abolitionists, the Russian writer Maxim Gorky— persona non grata elsewhere in town because of his Bolshevist views—all gave talks. The roster is starred with great names.

In its first year, the reading room, open to everybody, drew three thousand readers a week, ten percent of whom were women. It was kept open until 10 p.m. to accommodate working people, the people for whom the Union was designed. There were objections to this idea of educating the working classes. Cooper, who had had almost no formal education himself, ignored them. At the annual Union reception, hundreds lined up to shake his hand. Even Gustavus Myers in his muckraking *History of the Great American Fortunes* (1910) had nothing bad to say about him.

The lectures still continue, still free. The various schools—art, architecture, engineering—are free, prestigious and only slightly less difficult than Harvard to enter.

The entrance is on 7th Street, directly behind the statue of Peter Cooper by Augustus Saint-Gaudens. Inside there often are interesting exhibitions—free, of course.

No. 6 St. Mark's Place—the St. Mark's Baths, closed in the wake of the AIDS epidemic—is the rather improbable site of **JAMES FENIMORE COOPER'S** last home in this city. In his time, St.

Mark's Place was a quiet street of comfortable family houses. Peel away the boutique signs, and the architecture will occasionally give you the picture.

Cooper (1789–1851), no relation to Peter, was not a real New Yorker. Born into a Tory family in New Jersey, expelled from Yale for "frivolity," he married into another Tory family, the De Lanceys, and retired to farm in Cooperstown, New York, on his wife's money. When that ran out, he began to write.

His first book was a dreadful novel called *Precaution*, written in imitation of Jane Austen. As anyone who has read him can testify, Cooper had no talent for irony or delicate social satire. In time, he found his style: the historical novel—first, *The Spy*, a Revolutionary War story, then the successful *Leatherstocking Tales.*

Mark Twain made fun of Cooper's pompous prose. But under the layers of Victorian rhetoric was a storyteller and a man who felt true concern over the clash between the heroic life of the frontier and the shoddy civilization that was engulfing it.

Cooper the man was a crusty, contentious person, half eighteenth-century squire, half nineteenth-century Romantic, and at home in neither world. Like so many of his fellow writers (including his critic, Mark Twain), he despised the demagoguery and increasing materialism of the new democracy. He was a believer in democracy— the ideal 18th-century democracy—and he spoke out bluntly, honestly and critically in essays very few people have bothered to read.

No. 77 St. Mark's Place, a shabby house, redstone instead of brown, was for twenty years the home of the poet, **W. H. AUDEN** (1907–1973). He lived one flight up, and the bar downstairs was one of his favorite hangouts.

Wystan Hugh Auden, named after an obscure Saxon saint, was very attached to his name: "I'd be *furious* if I ever met another Wystan." He was born in York, England, but chose to live in New York—New York, he said, *not* the United States—and became an American citizen.

A tall, clumsy man with flat feet and bitten fingernails, he went about in a single suit until the pants split. He could reduce any interior to chaos in record time and lived in a welter of books, papers and empty bottles. Cigarette burns on tables were a sure sign of his occupancy. His flat feet hurt, so he wore carpet slippers (frayed) even with evening dress. At parties in the St. Mark's Place flat which he shared with his long-time lover, Chester Kallman, he served champagne, French for celebrities, California for the others; both vintages democratically cooled in the grimy bathtub and served in jelly jars.

Auden's eccentricities make good copy, but they are in no way the measure of the man. The essential Auden was brilliant, erudite, logical, moody and passionate. He had a fine sense of fantasy and fun, which never interfered with his work. He went to bed early, rose early, and wrote daily, something he considered absolutely necessary for producing good verse. The unadorned simplicity of his style is deceptive; as a technician he is unparalleled. He could, and did, write in any meter.

He had a second talent: friendship and love. When Thomas Mann's daughter, Erika, was on the run from the Nazis, she sent Auden a marriage proposal, although she had never met him. It was to be a marriage of convenience to give her British citizenship. Immediately, he telegraphed, "Delighted." "I'll probably never see her again, but she seemed very nice," he remarked after the ceremony.

Admittedly gay at a time when homosexuality was socially unacceptable, his relationship with Chester Kallman lasted until the end of his life. They lived and worked together, collaborating on various projects including the libretto for Stravinsky's opera, *The Rake's Progress.*

In middle age, Auden's handsome English schoolboy face collapsed into a map of suffering, crisscrossed with deep lines gouged out by an inner life lived at high intensity. He once told friends that he hoped God would take him away at seventy. He got his wish, with a bonus. He died in his sleep at sixty-six.

In the little stores along Second Avenue, his *Times* obituary was taped to many cash registers. The shopkeepers might not have read Auden's poems, but they knew him, and they valued him.

The bronze plaque on the facade of 77 St. Mark's Place quotes two beautiful lines of his:

> If equal affection cannot be
> Let the more loving one be me.

ST. MARK'S CHURCH-IN-THE-BOWERY, Second Avenue at 10th Street, was built in 1660 as a Dutch chapel on Governor Peter Stuyvesant's farm—"bowery" or "bouerie" means "farm" in Dutch. Stuyvesant is buried in the east churchyard wall.

The church is nominally Episcopal but with a long history of dissent. It functions as a real force in the neighborhood with its free Thanksgiving dinners, open to one and all, its faith-healing sessions, and its various cultural programs. The **POETRY PROJECT**, twenty years in existence and run by poets, is one of the city's leading forums for avant-garde poets, known and unknown. The weekly program of readings is posted on a bulletin board on the 10th Street church gates. Admission to a reading is $5.00; a yearly membership costs $50.00.

The East Village is full of young poets. One of their mentors is **ALLEN GINSBERG**, who lives in the neighborhood. The young Beat poet who caused a major sensation with the publication of his long poem, *Howl* (published in 1956, when he was thirty), is now a kindly middle-aged gent with a cane. "Uncle Gins," as his younger friends call him, currently writes blues poems which he sings to the accompaniment of a jazz sax.

YIDDISH THEATER. Second Avenue between Houston and 14th Streets once glittered as the "Jewish Broadway." By 1918 twenty theaters were presenting melodramas and musicals in Yiddish, mostly on immigrant themes that would appeal to the audiences. Schmaltz, by and large, but hardly more schmaltzy than the uptown commercial theater of the day.

Jacob Adler, dean of Yiddish actors, played Shakespeare. His *Jewish King Lear* was especially popular; audiences responded strongly to the familiar theme of family conflict. Adler was the first to play Shylock as a proud, unbending, Old Testament Jew, a role he repeated on Broadway, speaking his lines in Yiddish while the rest of the cast spoke English. Adler founded a dynasty of distinguished actors. His children, Luther and Stella, helped found the Group Theatre of the 1930s and created roles in a series of plays by the young Clifford Odets: *Awake and Sing, Paradise Lost, Golden Boy.* Stella Adler went on to become one of New York's leading drama teachers, training Marlon Brando, among others.

The gathering place for these theater people and for the many Yiddish writers—poets, principally, who worked in the sweatshops by day and wrote verse by night—was the Café Royal, in the heart of the Jewish theater district, on Second Avenue and 12th Street. The waiters observed the pleasant European custom of allowing one to linger all evening over a single coffee. Successful actors sat on the right; strivers on the left. For a small tip a waiter would page an unknown for a nonexistent phone call—poor man's publicity.

The Second Avenue Delicatessen on the corner of Second Avenue and 10th Street is famous for its corned beef and pastrami, its soups, and its "specials"—fat frankfurters that spurt when you stick your fork in. It's kosher, so no mixing of meat and dairy. Don't ask for cream in your coffee or cheese in your sandwich. The sidewalk in front is a concrete bed of stars, each bearing the name of a Yiddish theater great.

BOOK ROW, an hypnotically fascinating line of secondhand bookstores, all with bargain bins in front, once extended up Fourth Avenue from Astor Place to 14th Street. During the last decade, as rents doubled, then tripled, the stores closed one by one, and one of New York City's great delights vanished.

For used books there are at present the Pageant Book & Print Company on 9th Street, just east of Fourth Avenue (you may recognize the facade: Woody Allen used the store for a scene in *Hannah and her Sisters*), and the Strand, Broadway at 12th Street. This huge warehouse of used books is doing big business and has 150 people on the payroll. The atmosphere is madhouse. The enormous stock makes it hard to get the specialized attention needed for hunting down elusive titles. On weekends the entire population of New York seems to converge on the premises, buying and also selling their own used books.

Many little bookstores are sprinkled throughout the East Village streets; many close before they have really opened. The St. Mark's Bookshop at 12 St. Mark's Place has, on the contrary, expanded. It specializes in small-press books, philosophy, and women's studies. Directly across the street at No. 13 is an annex where you can find sale books and "little" magazines.

Fly-by-night unlicensed peddlers along St. Mark's Place between 3rd and 2nd Avenues are attempting to recreate Book Row. Laid out on the pavement you will find everything from choice art books to discarded school texts.

St. Mark's Place

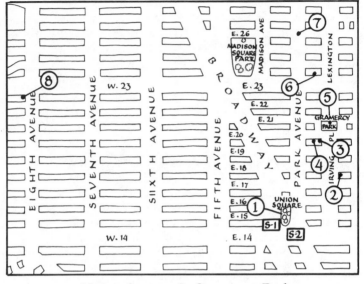

Union Square & Gramercy Park

1. Union Square
2. Pete's Tavern
3. Players Club
4. National Arts Club
5. Gramercy Park
6. Kenmore Hotel (Crane and West)
7. Melville Square
8. Chelsea Hotel

Union Square & Gramercy Park

Subway Stops: S-1. 14th Street (BMT)
S-2. 14th Street (East Side IRT)

UNION SQUARE has seen a lot of history. Union troops departed from here during the Civil War; hence its name. In the 1930s it was the center of New York's radical movement: the park was a forum for soapbox speakers, the May Day parade traditionally ended up here, the Communist *Daily Worker* had offices nearby on 13th Street. Artists and writers lived in the 14th Street lofts facing the square. S. Klein's enormous store on the square's eastern side was purveyor of cut-rate fashions to the proletariat. Beggars, pretzel sellers, unlicensed peddlers who packed up and fled when a cop came in view were everywhere. Movie houses showed Soviet films. Fourteenth Street belonged to New York's working people. Albert Halper's best-selling novel of the 1930s, *Union Square*, will give you a complete picture.

Union Square today is quiet, refurbished, prettied up with an art nouveau subway entrance. The lunch crowd eats Big Macs on the park benches. During warm weather, a lively "green market" flourishes at the northern end. Klein's is gone, replaced by an enormous and enormously expensive Zeckendorf condominium. Fourteenth Street remains a cheap and lively shopping street, full of bargains that are no bargains. Turn east from 4th Avenue into 17th Street for Gramercy Park.

The **GRAMERCY PARK** neighborhood, tucked away behind Union Square, is one of those surprises only big cities offer: a quiet residential square isolated in the heart of strident New York. The park was created by Samuel B. Ruggles, an early real estate

developer. In 1831 he drained marshland, laid out the streets and
the central square on the English pattern, then offered lots for sale
to the gentry. A big inducement was the locked park, keys handed
out only to owners of property on the square. Fortunate children,
whose parents have possession of the key awarded to "suitable"
neighborhood residents, still play in security behind the tall iron
gates under the shadow of the statue of Edwin Booth as Hamlet.

A circle of fine old buildings surrounds the Park. On the south
(downtown) side at No. 15 is the **NATIONAL ARTS CLUB**, founded
in 1896 with the aim of uniting literature and the other arts. From
the first it broke with convention and admitted women to
membership.

Next door at No. 16 is the **PLAYERS CLUB**, founded in 1888 by
Edwin Booth, who hankered after respectability for himself and his
fellow actors. To save them from a bohemian fate, he bought the
building and hired the great New York architect Stanford White to
remodel it. Booth lived in rooms at the club, and to his undying
delight the membership grew to include such irreproachables as
Mark Twain and Civil War General Sherman. As for Stanford
White, who had made the club so attractive, he was a darling,
beloved by his many friends, but certainly not respectable. He was
shot down by an irate husband, millionaire Harry Thaw, who was
insanely jealous of White's kinky relationship with his wife, the
beautiful Floradora chorus girl, Evelyn Nesbit.

Literary people of the more genteel sort flocked to the Gramercy
area. The atmosphere was more intellectual than bohemian, quite
different from Greenwich Village. **HERMAN MELVILLE**, who was
neither genteel nor bohemian, but hard up and generally
disenchanted with life, lived nearby in a dismal row house on East
26th Street, a sort of no-man's-land, not quite Gramercy and not
quite anything else. A sign at the corner of Park Avenue South and
26th announces that this is Melville Square. He wrote *Billy Budd*

in his dreary bedroom, wrote it for himself, since he had long lost faith in the public. The manuscript was found among his papers after his death and went on to glory.

RICHARD GILDER (1844–1909), editor of the all-powerful *Century* magazine and a good minor poet, lived in a little house, "The Studio," once Samuel B. Ruggles's stable, at 103 East 15th Street (now a small office building). The *Century* had grand offices with Persian carpets on Union Square. Gilder befriended and published many of the major writers of his day. He serialized *Huckleberry Finn*—with expurgations—which infuriated the literati with the exception of its author, who accepted them with good grace. Talk about controversial novels! *Huck Finn* has *Ulysses* and *Lady Chatterley's Lover* beat by at least half a century. Our American masterpiece was, is, possibly always will be in trouble with some sort of censor.

Gilder also published chunks of Henry James's *The Bostonians* and *The Rise of Silas Lapham* by **WILLIAM DEAN HOWELLS** (1837–1920), a great gun in his time. Howells left Boston and the editorship of the *Atlantic Monthly* for New York and came to live on East 17th Street. The color and variety of the city engulfed him. He liked riding the elevated railways—the "els"—which darkened and contaminated the major avenues. He walked the neighborhoods—a great New York sport—and was among the first to understand and sympathize with the problems of the Lower East Side. *A Hazard of New Fortunes,* published in 1890, was one of the first realistic novels about New York.

O. HENRY (1862–1910)—William Sidney Porter—North Carolinian by birth, jailed embezzler, newspaperman, and America's most durably popular writer of short stories lived happily on Irving Place. The *New York World* paid him $100 apiece for his stories, which afforded him a comfortable flat with a fireplace. After a grim, hunted life, he was glad to come to rest in "Baghdad on the

Subway," as he called New York. His favorite bar, Healy's (now Pete's Tavern), was nearby on 18th Street, and O. Henry liked his booze. There's a plaque over a booth at Pete's announcing that O. Henry wrote his most famous story, *The Gift of the Magi*, on this spot. His nocturnal strolls soon became famous. He crisscrossed the city in search of new neighborhoods and story ideas accompanied by an army of writer-fans, including Franklin P. Adams, later F.P.A. of Algonquin Round Table fame.

O. Henry is out of fashion now, his sentimental stories with trick endings relegated to high school English classes. He repays rereading for his pictures of New York as it was—a world of hall bedrooms in cheap rooming houses, starving artists, underpaid shopgirls (a word he detested: "Call them girls who work in shops," he said). He wrote about ordinary people, their pleasures and problems, with true kindliness and humor, and always with understanding.

STEPHEN CRANE (1871–1900) lived in a studio at 145 East 23rd Street with three artist friends, all of them so broke they shared one bed. He was the son of a Methodist minister from Newark, New Jersey (ministers seem to have produced half this country's

Union Square

writers), and a mother who lectured and wrote. The family was conventionally pious but with high standards and brains, which they bequeathed to their youngest son in the form of a blazing, original and precocious talent.

By the age of twenty-one Crane had written *Maggie: A Girl of the Streets,* a bombshell of a novel set in The Bowery, a name which still rings alarm bells. The Bowery is now only a bleak continuation of Third Avenue south of St. Mark's Place, lined with restaurant supply shops and New York's ever-increasing homeless population. In Crane's day it was notorious: a gaudy pleasure palace for the poor, a titillating bit of low life for the "swells." Crane, who was always attracted by low life, lived for a while in a Lower East Side rooming house, walked the streets, poked into the abominable alleys, drank in the gaslit saloons and gathered his material.

Maggie is the story of the downfall of a pretty, gentle tenement-and-sweatshop girl, born into a jungle in which only predators can survive. Less than a hundred pages in length, told in a series of lightning-flash episodes anticipating the jump-cut technique of today's filmmakers, it was an affront to the literature of the time. No other American realist had been quite so merciless. The *Century* rejected the manuscript as "too cruel." "Too honest, you mean," Crane shot back. He was always very self-confident. He had to be. Nobody wanted to publish the book. At length he took the scrapings of his inheritance from his father and had *Maggie* privately printed under the pseudonym Johnston Smith. The printer cheated him. He was penniless and about to give up literature when word reached him that William Dean Howells had read the book, liked it and was prepared to say so in print. Crane went on to write *The Red Badge of Courage,* a war novel written from the point of view of a very young, very green soldier. No heroism, no blood and guts, only the confusion of a smoke-filled battlefield and the helplessness of a boy caught in the machinery of war. It could have been written about Viet Nam. The book was published and acclaimed. Crane had arrived. He was twenty-four, thin and coughing, but as always, ignoring his health.

He went all the way West, then to Mexico, wrote a series of magnificent short stories, then on to England with his girlfriend, the ambitious Cora, who was passed off as Mrs. Crane. He made friends with Joseph Conrad and Henry James, lived opulently and beyond his means. Then death, coughed out with TB, at the age of twenty-nine.

NATHANAEL WEST (1903–1940) was night clerk at a Gramercy Park hotel, the Kenmore Hall, now a seedy welfare hotel located on the site of Stephen Crane's old rooms at 145 East 23rd Street. West had graduated from Brown and gone to Paris in the great expatriate days. Returning to the States in Depression times, he was glad to get any job at all. The Kenmore Hall stint worked very well for him. He was able to write on the job, and he could treat his friends to lunch and a swim in the hotel pool. Dashiell Hammett, then an impoverished writer for the detective pulps, had a room at the Kenmore. When he faced eviction for nonpayment of rent, West arranged for him to stay on under a false name. When once again his credit ran out, he skipped, with West's collaboration.

West's best friend was his fellow student from Brown and brother-in-law, S. J. Perelman. It was Perelman who introduced him to the lovelorn columnist of the *Brooklyn Eagle*. The desperate, semiliterate letters she received fascinated West. From them, the idea for his novel, *Miss Lonelyhearts*, was born. His first novel, *The Dream Life of Balso Snell*, had mystified both the critics and its few readers with its surreal literary style. *Miss Lonelyhearts* is written in straight, matter-of-fact prose, which makes the book even more grotesque and terrifying. "Miss Lonelyhearts" is a young newsman saddled with the chore of the lovelorn column. Letter by letter he becomes more enmeshed in the tragedies of his correspondents, until he, too, becomes a casualty. The book was well received, but West's publisher went broke; only a hundred copies sold, and West took off, like so many of his contemporaries, for Hollywood.

He did nothing for the movies, but he did produce a fine

Hollywood novel, *The Day of the Locust:* not the Hollywood of stars and producers, but the town of hangers-on, grotesques and failures—a worm's-eye view of Movieland.

West died on the threshold of his career, killed in a car crash with his bride of a few months, Eileen McKenney, the Eileen of her sister Ruth's famous multimedia opus. Perelman was his literary executor and did a good job of it. From underground cult novelist, West has become a major American writer. Generation after generation seems to rediscover and understand him.

S. J. PERELMAN (1904–1979) was—and still is—the most brilliant, most original humorist this country has produced: far more brilliant (on paper, at least) than any Algonquin Round Table wit. As he wrote, "Before they made Perelman, they broke the mold."

Born in Brooklyn, Perelman grew up on a failing chicken farm near Providence, Rhode Island, left Brown University without a degree (trouble with trigonometry) and settled in Greenwich Village. The *New Yorker* discovered him and continued to publish him throughout his long career. His greatest fame, however, comes from his collaboration with the Marx Brothers, which resulted in the film classics, *Monkey Business* and *Horse Feathers.* His relationship with the formidable four (later, three) was often vituperative. "We had good writers; he wasn't one of them," said Groucho ("Cuddles," to Perelman.) Perelman retaliated by calling the Brothers "boorish" and "megalomaniacal." With old age, they softened and admitted each other's virtues.

Perelman's long and far-from-happy marriage with West's sister, Laura, lasted until her death. He then moved to London "forever" and came back in a few years. He spent his last years, not in Greenwich Village, but as a resident of the Gramercy Park Hotel at 2 Lexington Avenue.

EDITH WHARTON (1862–1937) belongs to Gramercy Park by background rather than physical presence. Her parents, the chic, well-connected George Frederick Joneses, lived in a house on East

21st Street, but by the time their youngest, named Edith, was born they had moved to larger, grander quarters on West 23rd Street.

West 23rd is one of the dullest streets in the city today, an endless stretch of second-rate office buildings. At 8th Avenue there is a single oasis: the **CHELSEA HOTEL**. This charming, down-at-the-heels establishment is infinitely tolerant of eccentricity (boa constrictors welcome), inability to pay (the lobby is hung with paintings presented in lieu of room rent), and unconventional hotel morality (prostitutes mingle freely with artists, writers and rock stars). Thomas Wolfe wrote *You Can't Go Home Again* here; Dylan Thomas spent his last alcoholic days in one of the rooms; Sid Vicious of The Sex Pistols and his girlfriend Nancy both died here under dreadful druggy circumstances. The Chelsea has bridged the generation gap. It fills a real need in a city like New York.

Edith Jones was born into quite another 23rd Street. A "good address," Old New York, three sets of curtains to fashionably darken the parlor, six-course dinners. She was intelligent and lonely; a reader and from early youth a writer; odd, but not quite a misfit. She married early in the approved manner, selecting a suitable young man, the amiable, good-looking Teddy Wharton. The marriage was immediately queered by Mrs. Jones's refusal to explain the facts of life to her innocent daughter. The consummation took three weeks. Edith was sexy enough in later life, but things never quite worked out with Teddy.

The young Whartons lived by their engagement book: they traveled extensively, summered in Newport, entertained handsomely. Edith, however, continued to write and even sell a piece here and there, a rather shameful achievement for a young society matron. Her first major success was the novel, *The House of Mirth*, the story of Lily Barth, a poor but well-born girl whose unconventional behavior loses her the chance for a good marriage and who is destroyed by the rigidly conventional society whose rules she has broken.

Edith was made of sterner stuff. She managed to surround herself with a group of compatible literary friends; Henry James was perhaps the dearest. Her grand summer house, The Mount, in Lenox, Massachusetts, a comfortable, beautifully appointed place, open to the public now, was always full of interesting guests.

In her middle forties, she made the break. She left Teddy and moved to Paris, where she soon conquered the usually impenetrable Faubourg St. Germain, that bastion of the old guard which occupied the sensibilities of Balzac and Proust. She was happy in Europe, quite understandably in view of the raw, philistine America of her time, which drove out so many of its able artists. She became a great hostess, took lovers, wrote and traveled incessantly. In 1920 she won the Pulitzer Prize for *The Age of Innocence,* which sums up her feeling for the New York she was born into: critical yet fond.

She finally divorced her husband and lived on in France, a formidable grande dame, impossible and unpredictable. One of the last persons she received was Sinclair Lewis. She had liked *Babbitt*—understood it, too. The rigid codes of Zenith, Ohio, were not so very different from those of her own New York.

Gramercy Park

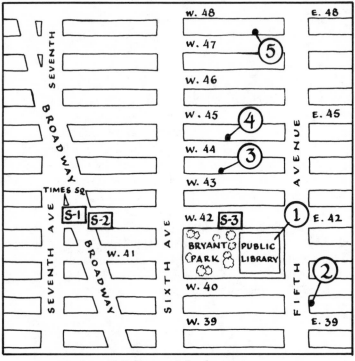

Midtown Manhattan

1. New York Public Library: Central Research
2. New York Public Library: Mid-Manhattan Branch
3. The *New Yorker*, 25 West 43rd Street
4. The Algonquin Hotel, 50 West 44th Street
5. The Gotham Book Mart, 41 West 47th Street

Midtown

Subway Stops: S-1. 42nd Street (IRT)
S-2. 42nd Street (BMT)
S-3. 42nd Street (IND)

THE NEW YORK PUBLIC LIBRARY. That huge building on Fifth Avenue at 42nd Street is the New York Public Library's Central Research Branch. The lions that guard the Fifth Avenue entrance are very precious to New Yorkers. Mayor Fiorello LaGuardia, of equally precious memory, named them "Patience" (downtown lion) and "Fortitude" (uptown lion) after the two virtues he believed most necessary to Americans during the difficult Depression years. During the Christmas season they wear wreaths around their Art Nouveau necks.

The building, which opened its doors in 1911, is the refuge of scholars, students, and people who want to get in out of the weather. Room 315, the Main Reading Room, has computerized book-finding, long reading tables and surprisingly comfortable wooden armchairs. Various sublibraries are scattered throughout the building—Judaica, Magazines and Periodicals, Science and Technology, a Map Division, to name a few. There is no longer a circulating library. To take out a book, you go to one of the branches: the nearest is Mid-Manhattan, almost across the street. The dance and theater collection is up at Lincoln Center at the Performing Arts Research Library, 65th Street and Amsterdam Avenue. The Schomburg Center for Research in Black Culture on Lenox Avenue has the world's largest collection in its field. More about the Schomburg on page 57.

Central Research, Performing Arts and Schomburg, with their constant and superb exhibitions, can be classified as museums as well as libraries. Central Research gives free guided tours, Monday through Saturday, at 11:00 a.m. and 2:00 p.m. The gift shop sells, among other things, library lion bookends, and during the summer months there is an outdoor café at Fifth Avenue, under the lions, where you can have a drink or a snack after your labors.

THE NEW YORKER. 25 West 43rd Street, a modest office building on a quiet side street, is the home of the *New Yorker*. The magazine began inauspiciously as the flop of 1925, a year notable for successes. It survived, unchanged. It continues, unchanged—no masthead, no letters to the editor column. A few years ago a table of contents was added as a sop to readers. Its list of contributors reads like the syllabus for a course on twentieth-century literature: J. D. Salinger; John Hersey, whose *Hiroshima* was printed complete in a single issue; I. B. Singer, who was presented to the English-reading public long before he became Singer, the Nobel Laureate; Truman Capote, whose *In Cold Blood* and other works appeared first in these pages; and, most particularly, its roster of humorists—Dorothy Parker, Robert Benchley, James Thurber, the inimitable S. J. Perelman.

The magazine was the idea of one man, Harold Ross, a tall, shambling young journalist fresh from the *American Legion Weekly*. His prospectus announced that the *New Yorker* would not be for "the Old Lady from Dubuque." Yet Ross himself was no city sophisticate. Haphazardly educated, suspicious of writers and big words, endowed with an almost Victorian modesty (which never inhibited his outbursts of profanity), he took a staunch position as resident Philistine. Any manuscript he read—and he read them all—bristled with basic queries: "Who he?" or "Don't get." Fancy writing got a withering, "Just monkeying around here."

"Hell, I hire anybody," he was fond of saying. He was always looking for a new "Jesus," his word for genius. The original Jesus was the great E. B. White, for years a mainstay of the magazine, writing most of "The Talk of the Town," convincing Ross that the drawings Thurber made for fun and tossed into the wastebasket were publishable, inventing titles for the "newsbreaks"—those back of the book tidbits, "Neatest Trick of the Week," etc., without which the *New Yorker* would not be the *New Yorker*.

Ross remained editor until his untimely death in 1951, when his long-time assistant, William Shawn, took over. Shawn retired in 1987, and the new publishers appointed Robert Gottlieb, a Knopf editor, in his place, without staff approval. Petitions, resignations, daily newspaper stories, general reader alarm followed. Gottlieb has stayed on. Despite dire predictions, the *New Yorker* still seems to be—the *New Yorker*.

THE ALGONQUIN AND THE ROUND TABLE. Pleasant and unostentatious, the Algonquin Hotel, 50 West 44th Street, is a favorite with visiting writers and actors. The lobby with its comfortable chairs and little tables is a fine place for an after-theater drink, and the food is better than most hotel food. The place hasn't changed much since the 1920s when the Round Table convened daily for lunch at a round table, stage center, in the Rose Room, the main dining room.

The regulars at this formidable gathering of wits included Dorothy Parker, Robert Benchley, Franklin P. Adams, Heywood Broun, Alexander Woollcott, playwrights George S. Kaufman and Marc Connelly, and a smattering of actors, when in town: the young Tallulah Bankhead, Noël Coward, Harpo Marx, for once in a speaking role. People tried to reserve nearby tables in the hope of overhearing a quip, an epigram, any shred of the brilliant verbal byplay that everybody was talking and reading about.

The Round Table was never a club. Its members were linked by compatibility. They were all young, bright, talented, doing good work. They met for lunch, at first because they enjoyed each other's company and needed it after a lonely morning in front of the typewriter or studying a part. Later, they undoubtedly rather enjoyed performing for their public—and for each other.

DOROTHY PARKER (1893–1967) attracted most attention. In her day every good or not so good bon mot that made the rounds was attributed to her. She was a tiny, pretty young woman with a disarmingly feminine manner and a gently killing tongue. Her poems and short stories still make the anthologies of American literature. As Constant Reader, book critic for the *New Yorker,* her one-line review of *Winnie the Pooh,* "Tonstant Weader fwode up," still warms unsentimental hearts.

Parker's best friend was **ROBERT BENCHLEY** (1889–1945), kindliest of wits, literary champion of the bumbling man. He was a good friend to Parker, resigning from *Vanity Fair* when she was fired after panning Billie Burke, wife of all-powerful Florenz Ziegfeld, in one of her theater reviews. As freelancers they shared an office known as Park Bench. Benchley later went to Hollywood and did well playing his own friendly bumblers in the movies. His short, "How to Sleep," a choice tidbit to watch for in rerun houses, won an Oscar.

ALEXANDER WOOLLCOTT (1887–1943) is forgotten today. He was once a coast-to-coast celebrity: drama critic on the *Times;* the Town Crier of his radio program, which acquainted millions with his mannered, high-pitched voice. Sentimental, melodramatic, adder-tongued, he was the model for Sheridan Whiteside in George S. Kaufman's *The Man Who Came to Dinner* and the inspiration for Ernie Kovacs's *Percy Dovetonsils.*

FRANKLIN P. ADAMS (1881–1960) was largely responsible for making the Round Table famous through his *Tribune* column, "The Conning Tower," in which he regularly reported the doings and sayings of "Mistress" Dorothy Parker and friends. There is nothing comparable to "The Conning Tower" in today's press. Gossipy, though certainly not a gossip column, witty, even erudite, all sorts of people read it. F.P.A. called himself "our own Samuel Pepys" and, emulating the seventeenth-century London diarist, gave a picture of a New York in the process of emerging as a world capital of sophistication.

The 1920s, like the 1970s, worshiped youth. The Round Tablers were not so very young, but they thought young and acted young. Prohibition was the law of the land but it never prevented them from drinking. The Algonquin was totally dry, but the hip flask solved that problem. Parker, whose emotional makeup was fragile (she attempted suicide a number of times and once received hospital visitors with ribbon bows covering her slit wrists), had a terrible tussle with alcohol. Benchley died before his time of cirrhosis of the liver. Both were committed liberals—Parker eventually went all the way left and joined the Communist Party. As a tribute to the struggle for justice and equality, she willed her entire estate to Martin Luther King. Benchley tried in vain to help the defense in the Sacco-Vanzetti trial by testifying to prejudiced remarks he had overheard their judge, Webster Thayer, make.

Recent revisionist biographies have implied that Round Table wit and wisdom has been wafted to us through an alcoholic haze. That's as may be. What remains incontrovertible is its charm, its intelligence.

BROADWAY AND DAMON RUNYON. Midtown Broadway is a neon jungle. The diminishing legitimate theaters occupy the side streets along with the infamous welfare hotels. Forty-second Street, "Crossroads of the World," is dying, but it's still the world's most famous sin street, all dope dealers, prostitutes of all ages and sexes, porno flicks and massage parlors. The Chicago writer, Nelson Algren, tried to capture the atmosphere in his final novel, *The Devil's Stocking.* If you like Algren or Zola or just want to view the lower depths from the volcano's edge, take a walk along 42nd from Broadway to 8th Avenue. Most people survive despite rumors to the contrary.

An earlier, more innocent Broadway was chronicled by **DAMON RUNYON** (1884–1946). He was an old-style newspaper man, a sports reporter who came to New York to work for Hearst. Broadway was his beat, as they say in old movies. Like many of his contemporaries, he was fascinated by the underworld. This was the prohibition era; bootleggers were household familiars who, if personable, got invited to the best parties. The petty gangsters, gamblers, race track touts and their girlfriends—the guys and dolls of the musical—accepted Runyon because he knew how to keep his mouth shut. He sat in on their get-togethers, imitated their fashions, spending thousands he could ill afford in sharp Broadway toggeries (no Brooks Brothers for Runyon), and married second time around a Broadway showgirl. He even had an uneasy friendship with a certain Mr. Brown, better known as Al Capone.

Runyon's stories haven't worn well. Their blend of humor and sentimentality is hard to take in today's context. The curious speech patterns and slang of his characters have vanished, along with the restaurants and clubs they frequented.

THE GOTHAM BOOK MART, 41 West 47th Street. "Wise men fish here," says the sign. This small bookshop has managed to defy the trend that is turning bookstores into supermarkets. It specializes in *Literature*: poetry, in and out of print, signed editions, 20th-century novels, books on theater and film. The staff is highly knowledgeable. The customers are interesting: bibliophiles, writers, lots of foreigners.

A detour to the Gotham will also give you a glimpse of one of New York's most fascinating business districts, the diamond center. Hitler drove the Jewish diamond cutters from Amsterdam; many of those who were lucky enough to escape settled here. Forty-seventh Street between 6th Avenue and Broadway is lined with jewelers, most of whom are housed in booths inside the big buildings. The show windows glitter with every sort of stone, diamond engagement rings predominating. The street is always crowded. Hasidic Jews in ear curls and black hats hurry along; a group gathers around a man who has unwrapped a handful of precious stones. An Eastern bazaar atmosphere, with the Gotham Book Mart doing business incongruously, but so felicitously, in the middle of it all.

The Algonquin Hotel

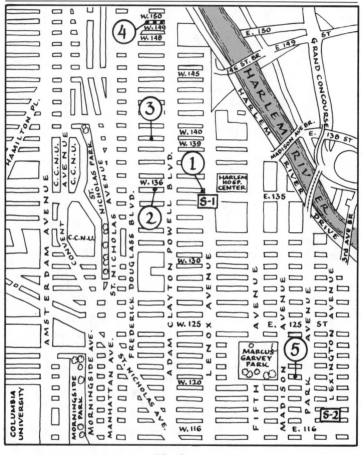

Harlem

1. The Schomburg Center
2. 108-10 W. 136th Street (A'Lelia Walker)
3. Strivers' Row
4. Dunbar Apartments
5. 20 East 120th Street (Langston Hughes)

Black Harlem

Subway Stops: S-1. 135th Street (IRT No. 2 or No. 3 train)
S-2. 116th Street (IRT No. 6 train)

A CITY within a city: multiracial, multilingual, poor, middle-class, rich. Art, crime, religion, protest, great educational institutions next door to slums, scholars and dope dealers, it's all here.

Spanish Harlem runs from East 110th to 116th Streets. Black Harlem is west, a huge neighborhood with a long history. Peter Stuyvesant established the village of Nieuw Haarlem in 1658. Dutch, French Huguenot, Scandinavian and German settlers came in and turned the land into lush farms. As the city grew, the farms gave way to streets of houses. Between 1910 and World War I a slump in real estate values opened the area to blacks, who came by the thousands, escaping the racial violence of the south and the poverty of the Caribbean and Latin America. Blacks displaced whites, creating a big-city sanctuary in a white-dominated world.

THE SCHOMBURG CENTER FOR RESEARCH IN BLACK CULTURE, Lenox Avenue at 135th Street, named after Arthur Schomburg, a black Puerto Rican bibliophile, is the best starting point for a Harlem walk. It is part of the city's public library system, and its vast collection—more than 100,000 volumes—includes such treasures as early editions of the works of the slave-poet, Phillis Wheatley, and the original manuscript of Richard Wright's *Native Son.* The Schomburg is also an art center; this is one of the best places to see paintings and photographs by black artists. Almost always, you will find a special exhibition illuminating some aspect of black culture on view. Admission is free. Open 12 noon to 8:00

p.m., Monday through Wednesday; 10:00 a.m. to 6:00 p.m., Thursday through Saturday.

The Schomburg grew out of the Harlem branch of the Public Library, where during the 1920s Ernestine Rose and her staff conducted poetry readings and book discussions that attracted city-wide attention. Later, during the 1930s, the building housed the WPA Writers' Project, which produced with the help of many then-unknowns a series of superb state and city guidebooks. *The WPA Guide to New York City* had Richard Wright and John Cheever on staff; all these decades later, in spite of many changes in the city, it is still one of the best introductions to New York.

Harlem never lacked black intellectuals; writers and artists as well as musicians have flourished here. The poet, **PAUL LAURENCE DUNBAR** (1872–1906), who never lived in the neighborhood, is commemorated by the Dunbar Apartments on West 149th Street, Harlem's first co-op, and the home of such famous people as Paul Robeson, Countee Cullen and W. E. B. Du Bois. **JAMES WELDON JOHNSON** (1871–1938), poet, lawyer, teacher, songwriter, had published his *Autobiography of an Ex-Colored Man* by 1912. Above all loomed the monumental figure of **W. E. B. DU BOIS** (1868–1963), scholar, teacher, writer, activist—the intellectual leader of black America. His pioneering study, *The Souls of Black Folk,* was published in 1903 and stated its point clearly: "The problem of the twentieth century is the problem of the color line." In 1903 this was an idea that had occurred to very few people. Throughout his long life, Du Bois remained a writer and a fighter. He was one of the key organizers of the NAACP and a founding father of what came to be known as the Harlem Renaissance.

The 1920s were years of cultural upheaval, and nowhere more than in Harlem, which saw an extraordinary flowering of literary talent. The dam simply burst. Black writers, forcibly silenced for centuries, began to speak out in novels, in essays, and especially in poetry.

The impetus for the Renaissance came from within. Two magazines, the NAACP's *Crisis* and the Urban League's *Opportunity*, had already published poems by **COUNTEE CULLEN** (1903–1946) before this twenty-year-old prodigy won an undergraduate Witter Bynner poetry award at New York University for his poem, "The Ballad of the Brown Girl." Cullen was a well-brought-up young man, the adopted son of a Harlem minister, Phi Beta Kappa at NYU. His poetry suited both blacks and whites: lyrical, wistful, not angry, obviously the work of an educated man, an educated black man.

When Charles S. Johnson, the editor of *Opportunity*, organized a literary symposium downtown at the Civic Club (the only unsegregated club of any stature in the city) and invited such white writers as H. L. Mencken, Eugene O'Neill and Carl Van Doren along with promising young black writers, Countee Cullen read his prize-winning poem. Van Doren gave the keynote speech. America needs black writers, was his message, and you are at this moment

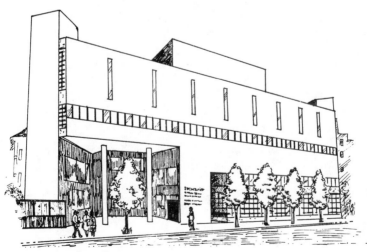

The Schomburg Center

in a strategic position to make your voices heard. Such optimism was new to his black audience, and it lifted them, quite literally, from their chairs. Shortly thereafter the black scholar and esthete Alain Locke published his essay, "Enter the New Negro," which declared the roots of the new writing to be purely American and emphasized the need for cooperation between "enlightened minorities," both black and white. Any thought of separatism was out.

Countee Cullen, who by then had published his first book of poems, *Color,* as well as received an M.A. from Harvard, was hired to edit *Opportunity*'s literary column, "The Dark (as opposed to ivory) Tower". He became a power on the literary scene, discovering new writers, printing contributions by the more established.

CLAUDE MCKAY (1890–1948) was a contributor to "The Dark Tower." Jamaican by birth, his early poems were written in Jamaican dialect. He came to the U.S. to study at Tuskegee Institute, which didn't suit him at all. He traveled on to New York to become co-editor of the avant-garde magazine, *The Liberator,* and to publish, in 1922, a collection of poems, *Harlem Shadows,* which made him a celebrity. He went on to England, became a Marxist; on again to the Soviet Union, where he was lionized, more for his blackness than his poetry. He was back in New York in time for the Renaissance. His novel, *Home to Harlem,* published in 1928, dealt entirely with Harlem low life and horrified the Renaissance elders, who tried to submerge the seamy side of Harlem in a flood of M.A.'s and Ph.D.'s. Du Bois declared that he felt like taking a bath after reading the book.

JEAN TOOMER (1894–1967), another "Dark Tower" contributor, wrote out of his own identity crisis. His ambiguous pen name is derived from Nathan Eugene Toomer. He looked white; by U. S. standards he was black because, like Dumas and Pushkin, he had some black ancestry. His grandfather had been a Louisiana lieutenant governor and a U.S. senator during the Reconstruction period. Toomer was brought up in Washington, D.C., in a middle-class white neighborhood. Handsome and gifted, he lived suspended between two worlds, belonging nowhere. "When I live with blacks, I'm a Negro," he told a friend. "With whites, I'm white, or better a foreigner." Writing *Cane*, a curious prose-poem novel, bought him a temporary measure of peace. He accepted, for a time, his black heritage. When he became a disciple of Gurdjieff, whose mysticism was fashionable during the 1920s, he left Harlem, stopped writing, disappeared into the cult.

ZORA NEALE HURSTON (1891–1960) was a "Dark Tower" discovery. She has been forgotten—ignored—for decades; now people are talking about her (maybe even reading her) again. She came to New York from Howard University in Washington, D.C., penniless but confident, largely because she won a prize in an *Opportunity* short story contest. Talented, a natural charmer and very ambitious, it wasn't long before she found herself hired as secretary to pop novelist Fannie Hurst, who didn't care that she couldn't type.

Zora Neale was very much of the younger Renaissance generation, challenging the proprieties of their elders, whom she called with wicked wit the "Niggerati"; the apartment she shared with several like-minded friends she referred to as "Niggerati Manor." Life didn't treat this young woman well. She continued to write and publish and also studied anthropology at Columbia under Franz Boaz. Her two folkway studies, one on Florida blacks, one on Haiti, went largely unread. Nobody was interested. She died broke and all alone.

LANGSTON HUGHES (1902–1967), from Missouri. Great poet, lovable man, Hughes was the crowning glory of the Renaissance and continued to shine long after its star had burned out. Like Hurston, he was younger generation and independent-minded. He rejected the gentilities of older black writers and wrote his poems in jazz rhythms. All of black experience—the disreputable as well as the respectable—fed his inspiration. "We younger Negro artists who create now intend to express our dark-skinned selves without fear or shame. If white people are pleased we are glad. If they are not, it doesn't matter. We know we are beautiful," he wrote in the *Nation*. This "manifesto" displeased the older generation, but Hughes had already made a name for himself with his first book, *The Weary Blues*, and it's hard to argue with success. He stayed on in Harlem, writing constantly, one of the great literary talents of his time. You can find the house he bought and lived in for twenty years at 20 East 120th Street.

Harlem's social life had never been dim, but under the Renaissance it absolutely scintillated; and it changed. White faces began to appear at parties. The leading hostess was A'Lelia Walker whose mother, Madame C. J. Walker, inventor of a hair-straightening product, had left her a million dollars and some valuable real estate. A'Lelia was no intellectual. When the conversation got deep she retired to the bridge table, but she did enjoy being a literary hostess, entertaining all sorts of people in her mansion at 108–110 West 136th Street, which was as elegant as any on the famous "Strivers' Row" on West 139th Street, a block of handsome Italianate townhouses done by Stanford White.

Always on hand was the white writer-photographer, Carl Van Vechten. It is difficult to be fair about such an individual today; a dilettante par exemple, chronicler of bohemia, ballet and blacks, he was full of good will but in retrospect most irritating. He became black-crazy. He wined blacks, dined blacks, adored blacks as "exotics," photographed blacks and ultimately wrote about blacks in a best-selling novel with the repellent title, *Nigger Heaven*. The vulgar term was not Van Vechten's metaphor for Harlem; it referred to the theater balcony from which he envisioned blacks looking down on and judging whites. Van Vechten's father tried to argue him out of the title. "I have never used that word in my life," he said, almost in tears. Nevertheless, it remained. The book lost Van Vechten a good many friends, and he found himself persona non grata at some of the nightclubs he was fond of frequenting.

Harlem in the 1920s was in fashion, a required stop on the tourist circuit. White parties thronged the nightspots to see the blacks "go primitive" when the drums began to beat. This new development was a nightmare for old-school Harlem intellectuals; their worst fears were coming true. The nadir was reached when the Cotton Club, Harlem's biggest, most popular nightspot, turned away W. C. Handy, who had come to hear Duke Ellington, while a party of (white) gangsters disported themselves at a ringside table.

The Depression snuffed out the Renaissance in the 1930s. Everybody was broke, Harlem brokest of all. Langston Hughes continued to write; his output was constant and enormous. In time, others came to take the place of the pioneers. They were better writers, freer—people like Richard Wright, James Baldwin and Ralph Ellison, whose novel, *Invisible Man*, won the 1953 National Book Award. The literary chain is unbroken; it has only lengthened and strengthened.

Harlem vending stand

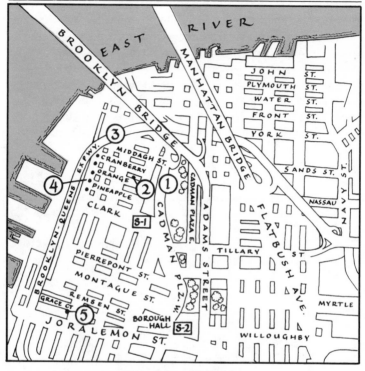

Brooklyn Heights

1. Site of *Leaves of Grass* printshop, at 98 Cranberry Street, now part of Cadman Plaza
2. Plymouth Church of the Pilgrims
3. Site of Middagh Street Commune at No. 7
4. Columbia Heights: No. 110 (Hart Crane), No. 111 (Thomas Wolfe), Nos. 124 & 142 (Norman Mailer)
5. 31 Grace Court (Arthur Miller)

Brooklyn Heights

Subway Stops: S-1. Clark Street (7th Ave. IRT)
S-2. Borough Hall (Lexington Ave. IRT)

THE RESIDENTS have a way of saying they live in Brooklyn *Heights,* as if the place were a floating island cut off from a mainland called Brooklyn. The Heights is undeniably special: an old, aristocratic New York neighborhood that has kept much of its character through the years. The best way to approach it is by walking over the Brooklyn Bridge. This way you will be able to examine close up the beauty of the bridge's spiderweb of steel cables and enjoy the panorama of the East River below.

In spite of the boutiques and restaurants that have sprouted during the last two decades, the neighborhood, with its quiet, tree-lined streets, its handsome brownstones and old frame houses, remains aloof from go-getting Manhattan (it is only fifteen minutes from Wall Street, where plenty of the inhabitants work). Writers have always liked the place. Arthur Miller lived on Pierrepont Street and later bought a house at 31 Grace Court, where he wrote *Death of a Salesman.* In 1951. he sold the house to W. E. B. Du Bois. Norman Mailer, Katherine Anne Porter, the poet Hart Crane, Truman Capote and Tennessee Williams all lived at one time or another on Columbia Heights, the choicest of all the choice streets. Here, back windows look out over little gardens to the wide sweep of the harbor. A broad esplanade runs beside the water and gives strollers the best view in town. At dusk, when the lights go on in Manhattan skyscrapers across the river, the power and beauty of the city is suddenly revealed in all its majesty.

This is a neighborhood of churches. The most famous is the Plymouth Church of the Pilgrims (Orange Street between Henry and Hicks). **HENRY WARD BEECHER** (Harriet Beecher Stowe's brother) was one of its ministers. Dickens spoke here; all the prominent abolitionists took the pulpit. Beecher was a great orator; he could outshout anybody, and he was dramatic. One Sunday he held a slave auction, putting a young black slave girl up for sale, and raised his congregation to such a pitch of indignation that they turned their pockets inside out to purchase her freedom.

WALT WHITMAN (1819–1892) is the Heights' most famous alumnus. As a young child he lived on Cranberry Street, across from the Plymouth Church. He was sent to Sunday school at St. Ann's on Clinton Street, more for the free lunch provided than the religious training. He followed Lafayette's carriage from Cranberry to Henry Street, where this last living Revolutionary War general had come to lay the cornerstone of a new library. All his life Whitman remembered being lifted up and kissed by the little old Frenchman who had helped us in our time of need.

By the time he was twelve Whitman was on his own. He worked for newspapers—errand boy, printer's devil, compositor, writer. At twenty-one he had worked for six or eight papers. He made it to the top, ending up in 1846 as editor of the *Brooklyn Eagle*; his vociferous opposition to the extension of slave states forced him out of the job.

Whitman was not always the "Good, Grey Poet," the gentle lion of the famous Eakins portrait. He was, after all, a newsman, in a day when newspapers were outrageous, scurrilous rags. Indolent, rakish, bohemian, sometimes a drifter, at other times very much Walter Whitman, Esquire, in his high collar and frock coat, he got to see every corner of the city. Loitering about or on a story, he took in the sights and sounds, felt the powerful rhythm of city life and stored it all away to reappear one day in what Emerson called "the book of the age," *Leaves of Grass*. No. 170 Fulton Street, corner of Cranberry, is the site of the printshop where Whitman in 1855 set up type for his masterpiece.

THOMAS WOLFE (1900–1938) escaped to a quiet apartment at 111 Columbia Heights when the sudden fame and adulation created by his first novel, *Look Homeward, Angel*, got to be too much for him.

Wolfe was a gigantic young North Carolinian, 6 feet, 4 inches or taller—so tall he used the top of his refrigerator as a writing table. His youth, good looks and wildly passionate writing style made him an immediate celebrity everywhere except at home. The citizens of Asheville, North Carolina, went into deep shock when they read *Look Homeward, Angel* with its autobiographical details and thinly disguised portraits of family and friends. "Sir: You are a son of a bitch," wrote one old lady who had known him all his life. People felt betrayed, but yet they had a sneaking pride in seeing a local boy make it, and make it big.

A number of publishers had turned the book down before Maxwell Perkins, Hemingway's and Fitzgerald's editor, read it and saw that the massive, disheveled manuscript (as massive and disheveled as its author) had extraordinary merit. He worked with Wolfe to reshape the novel; some three hundred pages were cut in the process. Perkins remained Wolfe's editor for years, guiding him through the later novels, *Of Time and the River* and *You Can't Go Home Again* (a title which has become a household phrase).

For a few years during the 1940s a group of writers shared an old brownstone at 7 Middagh Street, once one of the most attractive Brooklyn Heights streets. Intellectual striptease artiste GYPSY ROSE LEE finished her mystery, *The G-String Murders*, while in residence. Composer-writer PAUL BOWLES and his wife, writer JANE BOWLES, lived on the second floor. BENJAMIN BRITTEN worked at the piano he had set up in the parlor. People came and went as vacancies occurred. CARSON MCCULLERS, ailing, neurotic and talented (she had made a brilliant debut at the age of twenty-three with her novel, *The Heart Is a Lonely Hunter*), moved in, and later RICHARD WRIGHT arrived with wife and child. The house was furnished with hideous cast-off 19th-century furniture. There was a good cook and incompetent maid. Presiding over this establishment was the poet, **W. H. AUDEN**. He sat at the head of the table and announced the menu: "We have a roast, two vegs, a salad and a savory. There will be no political discussion." Order was thus maintained; there was no bickering, and the venture in communal living worked—a notable event.

Columbia Heights

Further Reading

Churchill, Allen. *The Improper Bohemians.* New York: Dutton, 1959. An entertaining informal history of Greenwich Village bohemia.

Howe, Irving. *World of Our Fathers.* New York: Harcourt Brace Jovanovich, 1976. The definitive history of the Jewish Lower East Side, with memorable drawings by Jacob (later Sir Jacob) Epstein, once an East Side boy himself.

Klein, Carole. *Gramercy Park, an American Bloomsbury.* Boston: Houghton Mifflin, 1987. A well-documented cultural history of the neighborhood from its beginnings to the present.

Lewis, David L. *When Harlem Was in Vogue.* New York: Knopf, 1981. A lively, well-written history of the political and cultural background of Harlem, its literary renaissance, its great years, and its popular decline.

Mitchell, Joseph. *McSorley's Wonderful Saloon.* New York: Duell, Sloane and Pearce, 1943. Fascinating essays on odd corners and odd people of New York, including Joe Gould.

Parrington, V. L. *Main Currents in American Thought.* New York: Dutton, 1927. A huge tome to read around in, Professor Parrington's essays on Fenimore Cooper, Twain and Melville are unparalleled. His notes on later writers, especially Crane and Cather, are sharp and to the point; only one real miss— Fitzgerald—whom he dismisses as "a short candle, already burned out"; but then, Parrington died in 1929 and had only Fitzgerald's first novel, *This Side of Paradise,* from which to judge.

WPA *Guide to New York City.* Prepared by the Federal Writers' Project of the WPA. New York: Random House, 1939. Fifty years have gone by since its publication, but it remains fresh, exciting, accurate. The unknowns who worked on the book (Richard Wright was one) not only got their facts straight, but captured the atmosphere, neighborhood by neighborhood.

Index